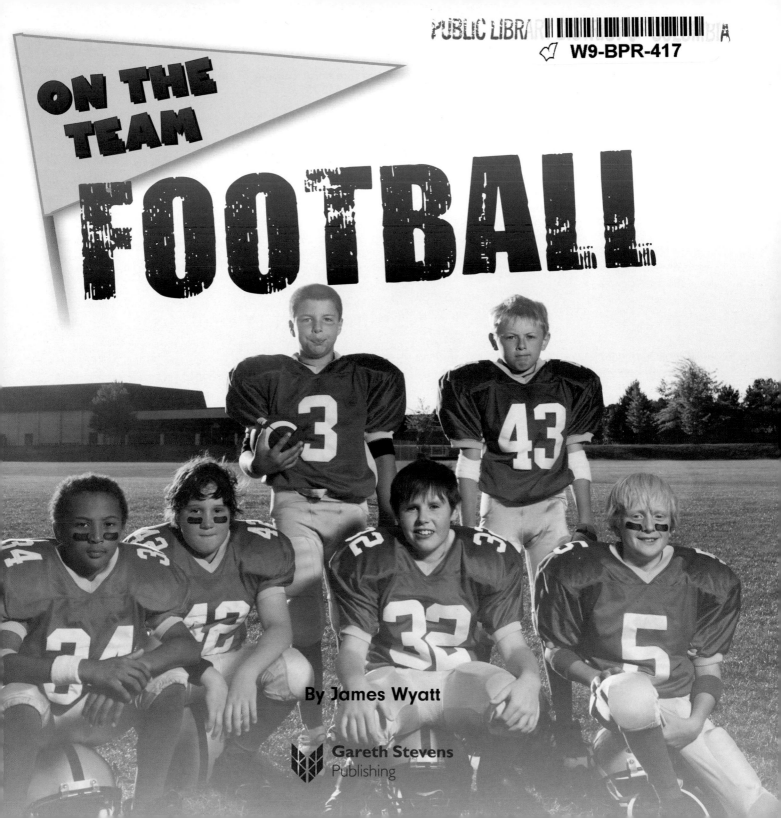

ON THE TEAM

FOOTBALL

By James Wyatt

Gareth Stevens
Publishing

Please visit our website, www.garethstevens.com. For a free color catalog of all our high-quality books, call toll free 1-800-542-2595 or fax 1-877-542-2596.

Library of Congress Cataloging-in-Publication Data

Wyatt, James, 1982-
Football / James Wyatt.
    p. cm. — (On the team)
Includes index.
ISBN 978-1-4339-6442-8 (pbk.)
ISBN 978-1-4339-6443-5 (6-pack)
ISBN 978-1-4339-6440-4 (library binding)
1. Football—Juvenile literature. I. Title.
GV950.7.W89 2012
796.332—dc23

2011023973

First Edition

Published in 2012 by
Gareth Stevens Publishing
111 East 14th Street, Suite 349
New York, NY 10003

Copyright © 2012 Gareth Stevens Publishing

Designer: Michael J. Flynn
Editor: Greg Roza

Photo credits: Cover, p. 1 Erik Isakson/Getty Images; pp. 5, 10, 13 (both), 14, 17, 20, 21 Shutterstock.com; p. 6 Chicago History Museum/Archive Photos/Getty Images; p. 7 Hulton Archive/Getty Images; p. 18 Fuse/Getty Images.

Printed in the United States of America

CPSIA compliance information: Batch #CW12GS: For further information contact Gareth Stevens, New York, New York at 1-800-542-2595.

Contents

Words in the glossary appear in **bold** type the first time they are used in the text.

Touchdown!

The game of football is often described as a battle between two armies. The offense tries to move the football forward to score points. The defense tries to push the offense back and take control of the football. Players on each team need to work together to score points while keeping the other team from doing the same.

Whether you play for your school or with your friends after school, football is a sport that requires players to come together as a team.

THE COACH'S CORNER

In many countries, the sport we call soccer is called football. People in those countries call the sport this book is about "American football."

Football players wear a helmet and a lot of pads. These keep the players safe during rough play.

Early football was a dangerous sport. In 1905, 18 players died! The rules were changed to make it safer.

This picture from around 1902 shows a high school football team in Chicago, Illinois.

Football's Founding Father

In the 1870s, Walter Camp created the first football rules. His game was based on the English game rugby, but it had several important changes. Camp added **downs**. He also added "scrimmage," which was a player handing the ball backward to another player to begin play.

Football became a popular sport in colleges across the country. Camp changed the rules over the years. He added the quarterback position and the forward pass. By the time Camp died in 1925, modern football had taken shape.

Walter Camp

On the Gridiron

Football is played on a grass field 100 yards (91 m) long and 53 yards (48 m) wide. Yards are marked along the sidelines. Lines crossing the field mark every 5 yards. These markings show teams how far they need to go to score.

A field has two end zones. The offense must have control of the football and get it into the other team's end zone to score a touchdown for 6 points. **Goalposts** stand on both ends of the field.

end zone

◄10

◄10

THE COACH'S CORNER

The offense has four downs, or tries, to go forward. If they can move forward at least 10 yards in four downs, they're given another four downs.

8

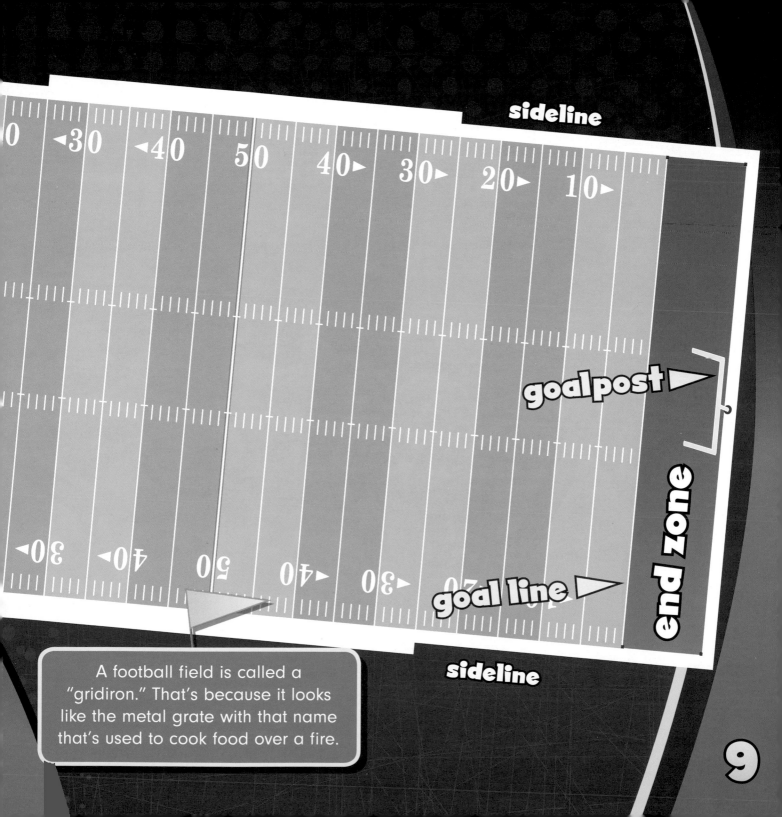

sideline

0 ◄30 ◄40 50 40► 30► 20► 10►

goalpost ►

end zone

goal line ►

sideline

A football field is called a "gridiron." That's because it looks like the metal grate with that name that's used to cook food over a fire.

9

quarterback

Before the snap, the quarterback uses code words to shout plays to the rest of the team so they know what to do.

Follow the Leader

Most scoring chances in football depend on the quarterback. This player leads the offense down the field. Each play starts when a player called the center **snaps** the ball to the quarterback.

Quarterbacks look quickly at the field and decide what to do. They can throw the ball to teammates or hand it to nearby runners. They can also run with the ball. Quarterbacks must be careful not to lose the ball or throw it to players on defense.

THE COACH'S CORNER

The players in front of the quarterback make up the offensive line. It's their job to stop the other team's defense from tackling the player with the ball.

Running and Catching

As important as quarterbacks are to the offense, they can't win games alone. They're surrounded by players who know how to take the ball and score. Running backs play behind the offensive line near the quarterback. They're fast players with great moves who run downfield with the ball.

After the snap, receivers run downfield and get ready to catch a pass from the quarterback. They run fast, jump high, and make diving catches. Running backs and receivers score with style!

THE COACH'S CORNER

Players on the offensive line help running backs and receivers. They run in front of those players and try to knock the defense out of the way!

running back

receiver

Receivers are often called wide receivers. That's because they usually line up far from the quaterback before the play begins.

Kickers need players called holders to keep the ball still while they kick for field goals and extra points.

Kicking and Punting

Sometimes the offense can't reach the end zone in four downs. That's when the team's kicker tries to kick the ball through the goalposts for a field goal, which is worth 3 points. Kickers do this to score an extra point after touchdowns, too. They also kick the ball to the other team after a touchdown.

When teams aren't close enough for field goals, punters kick the ball far down the field. They're good at punting high and aiming for open spaces.

THE COACH'S CORNER

Kickers and punters stand farther away from the center than the quarterback does. So, they need "long snappers" to send the ball back to them.

Playing Defense

The defense tries to stop the offense from scoring. They tackle players carrying the ball. When the defense tackles the quarterback, it's called a sack.

The defense tries to get the ball away from the offense. They can do this by knocking the ball out of another player's hands and then picking it up. That's a fumble. They can also **intercept** a quarterback's pass. Once they get the ball, the defense runs the other way and tries to score!

THE COACH'S CORNER

The defense can score 2 points by tackling a player on offense while they're in their own end zone. That's called a safety.

A team's defense can stop the other team from scoring and get the ball back.

17

During a football game, there can be up to seven officials on the field. They wear black-and-white shirts so they stand out from the players.

Don't Break the Rules!

Football players must play by the rules or their team will get **penalties**. When the defense is called for a penalty, the offense gets free yards or extra downs. When the offense is called for a penalty, they lose yards, which puts them farther from the end zone.

Football is a hard-hitting game, but players must be careful. The rules are made to keep players safe—and there are a lot of rules!

THE COACH'S CORNER

When a player breaks a rule, the referee throws a yellow flag onto the field. The referee then explains what the penalty is and who broke the rules.

In the Pros

Ask anyone who plays football, and they'll tell you it's a lot of fun. But it's hard work, too. Football players must be in good shape. They must train regularly, eat right, and get plenty of sleep if they want to help their team win.

Players who work the hardest may get the chance to play for a college team. If they do well in college, they may get the chance to play for a **professional** team in the National Football League (NFL).

Football Positions

Offense

quarterback	leads the offense, gets the ball to teammates who can score
running backs	run with the ball and score
receivers	catch the ball and score
center	snaps the ball to the quarterback and keeps him safe from the defense
tackles and guards	make up the offensive line; keep the quarterback, running backs, and receivers safe
tight ends	part of the offensive line, can catch the ball or help keep the quarterback and running backs safe

Defense

ends and tackles	make up the defensive line, rush at the quarterback and stop the running backs
linebackers	play behind the defensive line and help where they're needed
cornerbacks	stop receivers from catching the ball and make interceptions
safeties	play behind the linebackers and help where they're needed

Glossary

down: one play, or one try to move the ball forward

goalpost: Y- or H-shaped post at each end of a football field. Field goals and extra points are made by kicking the ball between the poles of a goal post.

intercept: to catch a pass that was supposed to go to the offense

penalty: a loss for breaking a rule

professional: earning money from an activity that many people do for fun

referee: an official who makes sure players follow the rules

snap: to send the ball back to the quarterback

tackle: to grab a player and force them to the ground

For More Information

Books

Doeden, Matt. *Play Football Like a Pro: Key Skills and Tips*. Mankato, MN: Capstone Press, 2011.

Jacobs, Greg. *The Everything Kids' Football Book*. Avon, MA: Adams Media, 2010.

Websites

NFLRush
www.nflrush.com
Play games and read the latest news about your favorite pro football team.

Rule Book: Beginner's Guide to Football
www.nfl.com/rulebook/beginnersguidetofootball
Read more about the basic rules of football.

Publisher's note to educators and parents: Our editors have carefully reviewed these websites to ensure that they are suitable for students. Many websites change frequently, however, and we cannot guarantee that a site's future contents will continue to meet our high standards of quality and educational value. Be advised that students should be closely supervised whenever they access the Internet.

Index

JUL 1 5 2014